Contents

Dedication 1
Preface 2
Chapter 1: Embracing the Entrepreneurial Spirit 6
Chapter 2: Finding Your Business Idea 13
Chapter 3: Building a Business Plan 20
Chapter 4: Funding Your Venture 27
Chapter 5: Marketing Your Business 34
Chapter 6: Developing Your Product or Service 41
Chapter 7: Legal Considerations 48
Chapter 8: Launching Your Business 55
Chapter 9: Managing Your Business 62
Chapter 10: Learning from Experience 69
Chapter 11: Inspiring Stories of Young Innovators 76
Chapter 12: The Future of Your Business 83
May I ask you for a small favor? 90
Book Summary 91
Acknowledgment 97

1.
2.
3.
4.
5.
6.
7.
8.
9.
10.
11.

12.
13.
14.
15.
16.

Dedication

To the fearless souls who dare to dream big,
This book is for those who have the courage to step off the beaten path, who believe in the power of their own potential, and who seek a life defined by purpose, passion, and freedom.

To the young visionaries starting out with bold ideas, to those reinventing themselves mid-journey, and to the late bloomers proving that greatness knows no age—may these pages give you strength, clarity, and the spark to pursue your dreams relentlessly.

And to my family, friends, and mentors—thank you for your unwavering support, for believing in me even when I doubted myself, and for reminding me that no journey is taken alone.

This is for all of you.

Preface

In a world brimming with untapped potential, *IGNITE-INNOVATE-LEAD* invites young dreamers and aspiring entrepreneurs to take charge of their futures, transforming ideas into impactful ventures. Whether you're a teenager taking your first steps into the entrepreneurial world or a parent seeking to nurture a young innovator, this book is your ultimate guide to embracing creativity, cultivating resilience, and building a business that matters.

With practical advice, inspiring real-life stories, and actionable insights, this book equips readers with the tools to tackle challenges head-on and turn passion into profit. From discovering your inner spark to mastering the art of problem-solving, every chapter is designed to guide you through the exciting and sometimes unpredictable journey of entrepreneurship.

What You'll Discover:

- The mindset of a true innovator: Learn how to overcome fear, embrace failure as a teacher, and harness creativity to solve real-world problems.
- How to spot opportunities: Find out how to identify market gaps, brainstorm innovative ideas, and validate them with real feedback.

- Building a solid foundation: Develop a business plan that sets clear goals, outlines strategies, and secures funding through creative avenues like crowdfunding, grants, and more.
- Marketing like a pro: Craft a compelling brand story, leverage social media, and connect with your target audience authentically and effectively.
- Legal and operational know-how: Understand the essentials of business registration, licensing, and creating a structure that works for you.
- Turning ideas into reality: Learn how to prototype, gather feedback, and continuously improve your product or service.
- The power of resilience and growth: Discover how to navigate setbacks, celebrate successes, and stay adaptable in a rapidly changing world.

But this isn't just a how-to manual. *IGNITE-INNOVATE-LEAD* features inspiring case studies of young entrepreneurs who defied the odds to create businesses that changed their lives—and the world around them. From nine-year-old Moziah Bridges, who launched a bow tie empire, to Mikaila Ulmer, whose lemonade business saves bees, these stories will show you that age is no barrier to success.

Whether you're dreaming of creating a business, solving a community problem, or leaving a legacy, *IGNITE-INNOVATE-LEAD* empowers you to take the leap. With each page, you'll uncover not just strategies and tips, but also the confidence to lead with purpose and passion.

Who This Book Is For:

- Adolescents curious about the world of entrepreneurship.
- Parents and educators looking to foster innovation and creativity in young minds.
- Anyone ready to ignite their entrepreneurial spirit and embark on a journey of self-discovery and growth.

This book is more than just a guide—it's a call to action. It challenges readers to look within, discover their unique potential, and share their brilliance with the world. Written in an engaging, motivational tone, *IGNITE-INNOVATE-LEAD* will leave you inspired, informed, and ready to take on the entrepreneurial world with confidence.

Join the Movement:
Get ready to unleash your inner innovator, turn your ideas into reality, and lead with purpose. Whether you're starting small or dreaming big, this book will ignite your passion, fuel your creativity, and empower you to make your mark.

Once you've read the book, we'd love to hear from you! Share your thoughts, leave a review, and join a growing community of innovators.

Your feedback not only helps us reach more aspiring entrepreneurs but also contributes to a world where creativity and innovation thrive.

Are you ready to ignite your spark, innovate fearlessly, and lead with impact?

The journey starts here.

Chapter 1: Embracing the Entrepreneurial Spirit

Understanding Entrepreneurship

Entrepreneurship is an exciting journey that involves taking an idea and transforming it into a reality. For adolescents, this journey can be particularly thrilling because it offers a chance to explore creativity, develop skills, and make a meaningful impact in their communities. Understanding entrepreneurship starts with recognizing that it's not just about starting a business; it's about solving problems and meeting needs. Every successful entrepreneur begins with a simple question: "How can I make things better?" This mindset encourages young innovators to think critically and creatively about the world around them.

At its core, entrepreneurship is about taking risks and embracing failure as a stepping stone to success. For young people, this can be a powerful lesson in resilience. Failure is not the opposite of success; it is part of the process. Each setback provides valuable insights and experiences that contribute to personal growth and development. By viewing challenges as opportunities to learn, adolescents can cultivate a strong entrepreneurial spirit that will serve them well in any future endeavor, be it in business or other areas of life.

Moreover, entrepreneurship fosters essential skills that are beneficial beyond the business realm. Skills such as problem-solving, communication, and teamwork are integral to any entrepreneurial venture. As young innovators embark on their projects, they will find themselves navigating various challenges that require collaboration with peers, seeking advice from mentors, and effectively presenting their ideas. These experiences equip adolescents with a toolkit of skills that will enhance their future academic and professional pursuits, making them well-rounded individuals ready to tackle any challenge.

Support from parents and mentors plays a crucial role in nurturing young entrepreneurs. Encouraging an entrepreneurial mindset at home can help adolescents feel empowered to pursue their ideas. Parents can foster this environment by engaging in discussions about innovation, supporting their children's interests, and even participating in projects together. By showing interest and providing guidance, parents can help their children navigate the ups and downs of entrepreneurship while reinforcing the idea that their aspirations are valid and achievable.

In conclusion, understanding entrepreneurship is an empowering journey for adolescents and their families. It opens doors to innovation, creativity, and personal development. With a focus on problem-solving, resilience, and skill-building, young innovators can embrace the entrepreneurial spirit and make a difference in the world. By encouraging exploration and supporting their ambitions, parents can help their children thrive in this exciting landscape, setting the stage for a bright and impactful future.

The Importance of Creativity

Creativity is a vital asset in the world of entrepreneurship. It serves as the driving force behind innovation, allowing young innovators to transform their ideas into reality. When you embrace creativity, you open the door to unique solutions and original products that can set you apart from the competition. In today's fast-paced market, businesses that thrive are often those that think outside the box and push the boundaries of conventional thinking. By nurturing your creative instincts, you can develop a mindset that is not only adaptable but also resilient in the face of challenges.

For adolescents, the journey of entrepreneurship is an exciting adventure that requires a blend of imagination and practicality. Creativity encourages you to envision possibilities that others may overlook. Whether it's brainstorming new business ideas or finding innovative ways to improve existing products, harnessing your creative potential can lead to groundbreaking opportunities. The ability to dream big and visualize your goals is an essential skill that will serve you well in both your business endeavors and your personal life.

Parents play a crucial role in fostering creativity within their children. By creating an environment that encourages exploration and experimentation, they can help young entrepreneurs discover their passions and talents. Simple activities such as engaging in arts and crafts, encouraging storytelling, or even allowing free play can ignite a child's imagination. When adolescents feel supported in their creative pursuits, they are more likely to take risks and embrace challenges, which are essential components of entrepreneurial success.

Moreover, creativity is not just about artistic expression; it is also about problem-solving. The entrepreneurial landscape is filled with obstacles, and innovative thinkers are often the ones who can find effective solutions. Developing a creative approach to problem-solving can empower young innovators to tackle issues head-on and turn setbacks into stepping stones. This skill is invaluable in business, as it enables you to pivot and adapt when faced with unforeseen circumstances, ensuring long-term sustainability and growth.

In conclusion, embracing creativity is fundamental for any aspiring entrepreneur. It fuels your passion and drives your ambitions, enabling you to carve out your unique place in the world. By nurturing your creative abilities, seeking support from parents, and viewing challenges as opportunities for innovation, you can lay the groundwork for a successful business venture. Remember, the journey of entrepreneurship is as much about the process as it is about the end result, and creativity will be your greatest ally along the way.

Identifying Your Passions

Identifying your passions is a vital first step on your journey as a young innovator. Passions are the driving force behind meaningful ideas, and they often provide the spark for entrepreneurial ventures. To discover what truly excites you, take a moment to reflect on the activities that make you lose track of time. Whether it's painting, coding, cooking, or organizing community events, these interests can reveal insights about your potential business endeavors. Keep a journal where you jot down what you love doing, as this will help clarify your thoughts and provide you with a roadmap to follow.

Engaging in various activities is an excellent way to explore your interests. Attend workshops, join clubs, or volunteer in your community. Exposure to new experiences not only broadens your horizons but also helps you identify what ignites your enthusiasm. Don't hesitate to try things that seem outside of your comfort zone; sometimes, unexpected experiences can lead to a newfound passion. Remember, every innovative entrepreneur has faced uncertainty, and it's through exploration that you will uncover your unique talents.

Discussing your interests with friends and family can also provide valuable insights. These conversations can spark ideas you may not have considered and help you see your strengths from an outside perspective. Ask them what they think you excel at or what they notice you enjoy the most. Engaging in constructive dialogue can inspire you and may even lead to collaborative opportunities where you can turn your passions into business ideas together. Embrace these discussions as a way to gain clarity and confidence in your entrepreneurial journey.

Once you have a clearer understanding of your passions, prioritize them. Not every interest will lead to a viable business, so focus on those that have the potential to grow. Consider how your passions align with market needs or gaps you've observed. This alignment can be the foundation of a successful venture. As you hone in on specific interests, think about how you can add value to others through your ideas. Remember, a successful business often stems from a genuine desire to solve problems or improve experiences for others.

Finally, don't be afraid to evolve your passions over time. As you grow and gain more experience, your interests might shift, and that's completely normal. Stay open to new possibilities and continuously seek inspiration. The entrepreneurial landscape is ever-changing, and your ability to adapt will enhance your journey as a young innovator. Trust in your instincts, embrace your passions, and take the first steps towards creating something that resonates with you and the world around you.

Chapter 2: Finding Your Business Idea

Exploring Market Gaps

Identifying market gaps is a crucial step for any young entrepreneur eager to make their mark. A market gap represents an unmet need or a demand that isn't fully satisfied by existing products or services. For adolescents and their parents, understanding how to recognize these gaps can lead to exciting business opportunities. Start by exploring your own interests and experiences. Consider the daily challenges you face or the activities that excite you. Often, the solutions to these problems can spark innovative business ideas that not only fulfill a personal need but also resonate with a wider audience.

Research plays a vital role in exploring market gaps. Encourage young innovators to dive into their communities and engage with potential customers. This can be done through surveys, interviews, or simply by having conversations with friends and family. Ask questions about their preferences, frustrations, and desires. This feedback can illuminate areas where products or services are lacking. Parents can support this process by helping their teens analyze the data collected, making it easier to identify patterns and validating the existence of a market gap.

Another effective approach is to study existing businesses and their offerings. Look for areas where competitors might be falling short. Perhaps there's a popular product that lacks certain features, or a service that isn't accessible to everyone. By evaluating what is available, young entrepreneurs can pinpoint opportunities for improvement or innovation. This analysis not only hones critical thinking skills but also fosters a mindset geared towards creative problem-solving, essential traits for any successful entrepreneur.

Networking and collaboration can also uncover hidden market gaps. Encourage adolescents to connect with peers, mentors, or local business owners who can provide insights into the industry. Attending workshops, community events, or entrepreneurial meetups can expose young innovators to diverse perspectives and experiences. These interactions can lead to brainstorming sessions that inspire new ideas or highlight needs that have yet to be addressed. Parents can play an active role by facilitating these connections and encouraging their children to step outside their comfort zones.

Finally, it's important to embrace experimentation and adaptability. Once a market gap is identified, young entrepreneurs should feel empowered to test their ideas. This could involve creating a prototype, launching a small pilot project, or even starting an online business. The journey may not always be smooth, but each step provides valuable lessons. Encouraging resilience and flexibility in the face of challenges will not only help young innovators refine their ideas but also build confidence as they navigate the entrepreneurial landscape. Emphasizing the importance of learning from mistakes can turn setbacks into stepping stones toward success.

Brainstorming Techniques

Brainstorming is a powerful tool that can unlock creativity and innovation in young minds. Whether you're trying to come up with a unique business idea or solve a problem, the right brainstorming techniques can make all the difference. One effective approach is to create a mind map. Begin with a central idea in the middle of a page and branch out with related thoughts, concepts, and potential solutions. This visual technique allows you to see connections and patterns that may not be immediately obvious, helping you explore different avenues for your business idea.

Another popular technique is the "free writing" method. Set a timer for five to ten minutes and write down everything that comes to mind about your business idea without worrying about grammar, spelling, or structure. The key is to let your thoughts flow freely. This exercise can help you break through mental blocks and tap into your subconscious creativity. After the timer goes off, review what you've written to identify any gems that stand out. You may discover insights that can lead to exciting new directions for your business.

Collaboration is also an essential part of brainstorming. Gather a group of friends, family members, or classmates and hold a brainstorming session. Encourage everyone to share their ideas, no matter how wild or unconventional. Create an atmosphere where all suggestions are welcomed, and build on each other's thoughts. This collaborative energy can spark new ideas and perspectives that you might not have considered on your own. Remember, the goal is to generate as many ideas as possible—quality can come later.

Consider using the "SCAMPER" technique, which stands for Substitute, Combine, Adapt, Modify, Put to another use, Eliminate, and Reverse. This method encourages you to look at your idea from different angles. For example, think about what you could substitute in your business model, or how you might combine two different ideas to create something new. By systematically applying these prompts, you can uncover innovative solutions and refine your business concept in unexpected ways.

Finally, don't forget to take breaks during your brainstorming sessions. Sometimes, stepping away from the problem can give your brain the space it needs to recharge and come up with fresh ideas. Engage in activities you enjoy, like playing sports, listening to music, or going for a walk. When you return to your brainstorming, you may find that your mind is buzzing with new thoughts and connections. Remember, the key is to stay curious and open-minded throughout the process—your next great business idea is just around the corner!

Validating Your Idea

Validating your idea is a crucial step before diving into the world of entrepreneurship. It's the process of checking whether your business concept has potential and if people are genuinely interested in what you have to offer. This phase can help you avoid unnecessary pitfalls and refine your idea based on real feedback. Remember, every great entrepreneur started with an idea, but it's the validation of that idea that often distinguishes success from failure.

Start by engaging with your target audience. Talk to friends, family, or peers who might benefit from your product or service. Ask them open-ended questions to gather their thoughts and feelings about your concept. Their insights can be invaluable and may reveal aspects of your idea that you hadn't considered. Don't be afraid to hear constructive criticism; it's an opportunity to learn and grow. This dialogue will not only validate your idea but also help you build a community of supporters who can champion your venture.

Another effective method of validating your idea is by creating a prototype or a minimum viable product (MVP). This doesn't have to be perfect; it just needs to showcase your concept. For example, if you're designing a new app, consider developing a basic version that highlights its core features. Share this prototype with your target audience, and observe their reactions. This hands-on approach allows you to gather direct feedback and make necessary adjustments. It also demonstrates your commitment to your idea, which can inspire confidence in potential customers and investors.

Leverage online tools and platforms to conduct surveys or polls. Websites like Google Forms or social media platforms can help you reach a broader audience beyond your immediate circle. Craft a simple survey that asks specific questions regarding your idea. Analyze the responses to identify trends and preferences. This data-driven approach can provide a clearer picture of market demand and help you refine your offerings further. Remember, the more information you gather, the more informed your decisions will be.

Finally, don't forget to embrace the power of networking. Attend workshops, webinars, or local entrepreneurship events where you can meet like-minded individuals. Sharing your idea in these settings can lead to valuable discussions and connections that may help refine your concept. Networking can also introduce you to mentors who have navigated the entrepreneurial journey and can provide guidance. By validating your idea through conversation, testing, and connections, you'll not only solidify your business concept but also build a strong foundation for your future endeavors.

Chapter 3: Building a Business Plan

What is a Business Plan?

A business plan is a dynamic document that outlines your business's goals, strategies, and the steps you will take to achieve them. It serves as a roadmap for anyone looking to start a business, providing clarity on what you want to accomplish and how you intend to get there. For young innovators, creating a business plan can be an exciting opportunity to transform your ideas into reality. It encourages you to think critically about your vision and the practical steps needed to bring it to life.

One of the key components of a business plan is the executive summary. This concise overview captures the essence of your business idea, highlighting what makes it unique and why it will succeed. As a young entrepreneur, this is your chance to showcase your passion and creativity. Think of it as your elevator pitch—a way to grab the attention of potential investors, mentors, or even friends and family who might support your venture. A compelling executive summary sets the stage for the rest of your plan and invites the reader to dive deeper into your ideas.

Another vital element is the market analysis, where you research and describe your target audience and competitors. Understanding who your customers are and what they want is crucial for any business, especially for young innovators eager to make a mark. This section encourages you to explore the needs and preferences of your audience and identify gaps in the market that your business can fill. By doing thorough research, you not only strengthen your business plan but also gain valuable insights that can guide your decision-making as you move forward.

The operational plan details how your business will function on a day-to-day basis. This includes everything from your location and facilities to the resources you need, such as equipment and staff. For adolescents, this is a chance to think about the logistics of running a business and how to effectively manage your time and resources. It's important to be realistic about what you can achieve and to outline the tasks necessary to keep your business running smoothly. This planning phase helps foster responsibility and prepares you for the challenges of entrepreneurship.

Lastly, a financial plan is essential for any business venture. This section outlines your expected income, expenses, and profitability. It might seem daunting, but understanding the financial side of your business is empowering. You'll learn how to budget, forecast, and potentially attract investors or secure loans. For young innovators, mastering these skills not only supports your current business but also lays a strong foundation for your future endeavors. Remember, every successful entrepreneur started with a plan, and your business plan is the first step toward bringing your innovative ideas to life.

Key Components of a Business Plan

A solid business plan is essential for any aspiring entrepreneur, as it serves as a roadmap for the journey ahead. The first key component of a business plan is the executive summary. This brief yet powerful section provides an overview of the entire plan, highlighting the business idea, market opportunity, and financial projections. Think of it as the trailer for a movie; it should capture attention and spark interest. A well-crafted executive summary can entice investors and persuade them to read further, so it's crucial to communicate your vision clearly and passionately.

Next, the business description offers a deeper dive into what your venture is all about. This section should detail your business's mission, vision, and goals. Describe the products or services you plan to offer and explain how they fulfill a need or solve a problem in the market. Make it relatable and inspiring; share your personal story or the inspiration behind your idea. This is your chance to connect with your audience, showing them the heart and soul of your business.

Market analysis is another vital component, providing insights into your target customers and the competitive landscape. By researching your potential market, you can identify trends, customer demographics, and the strengths and weaknesses of your competitors. This information not only helps you understand where your business fits in but also guides your marketing strategies. Don't shy away from sharing your findings; the clearer your understanding of the market, the more confident you will feel in your decisions moving forward.

The marketing and sales strategy section outlines how you plan to attract and retain customers. This is where creativity shines! Discuss your branding, promotional tactics, and sales channels. Whether it's social media campaigns, influencer partnerships, or community events, the options are endless. Young innovators should explore unique and innovative strategies that resonate with their peers. It's essential to demonstrate how you will engage your audience and build lasting relationships with them.

Finally, the financial projections section is where you lay out your plans for funding and revenue. This may sound daunting, but it's simply about making educated guesses based on your research. Include estimates for startup costs, sales forecasts, and break-even analysis. Being clear and realistic about your financial needs shows potential investors that you have done your homework and are serious about your business. Remember, every successful entrepreneur starts with a dream, and a well-structured business plan can help turn that dream into reality.

Setting Goals and Milestones

Setting goals and milestones is a crucial step for young innovators eager to embark on their entrepreneurial journey.

Goals provide direction and purpose, helping you clarify what you want to achieve. Whether it's launching a product, building a brand, or simply learning about business, having specific goals in mind will keep you focused and motivated.

Start by thinking about what excites you the most about entrepreneurship. Is it the idea of creating something new, or perhaps the prospect of solving a problem in your community? Identifying your passion will help you set goals that resonate with your interests.

Once you have a clear vision, break down your goals into smaller, manageable milestones. This approach makes the process less overwhelming and allows you to celebrate your progress along the way. For instance, if your ultimate goal is to launch a website for your business, you might set milestones such as researching your target audience, designing your website layout, and writing content for your pages. Each milestone achieved will not only bring you closer to your main goal but also boost your confidence and enthusiasm for the project.

It's essential to make your goals SMART: Specific, Measurable, Achievable, Relevant, and Time-bound. For example, instead of saying, "I want to make money," reframe it to, "I will sell 50 handmade bracelets online within the next three months." This transformation adds clarity and makes it easier to track your progress. By ensuring that your goals meet these criteria, you increase your chances of success and make it easier to stay committed, even when faced with challenges.

Involving others in your goal-setting process can also be incredibly beneficial. Share your aspirations with friends, family, or mentors who can provide support and accountability. They can offer valuable insights, share their experiences, and inspire you to push through obstacles. Creating a network of like-minded individuals who share your entrepreneurial spirit can significantly enhance your motivation and help you stay on track. Remember, you don't have to do this alone; collaboration can spark creativity and open new doors.

Lastly, be flexible and willing to adjust your goals and milestones as you progress. The entrepreneurial journey is often unpredictable, and you may discover new interests or face unforeseen challenges along the way. Embrace these changes as opportunities for growth. Regularly review your goals and milestones, and don't hesitate to adapt them to better align with your evolving vision. With determination, resilience, and a clear roadmap, you'll be well on your way to turning your entrepreneurial dreams into reality.

Chapter 4: Funding Your Venture

Understanding Startup Costs

Understanding startup costs is a crucial step for any young entrepreneur eager to launch their first business. These costs represent the initial investments required to get your venture off the ground and can vary significantly depending on the type of business you want to create. As you embark on this exciting journey, it's essential to grasp what these costs entail so you can plan effectively and avoid any unnecessary surprises down the road.

One of the first things you need to consider is the nature of your business. Are you planning to sell products, offer services, or develop a digital platform? Each of these paths comes with its own set of startup costs. For instance, if you're thinking about a product-based business, you'll need to account for materials, manufacturing, and possibly inventory storage. On the other hand, a service-oriented business might require less upfront investment but could involve costs related to marketing and tools needed to deliver your services effectively.

Next, think about operational expenses. These are the ongoing costs that keep your business running, including things like utilities, rent for physical spaces, or subscription fees for online services. Even if you operate from home, there might still be costs associated with internet services, software, or tools that facilitate your work. It's vital to create a comprehensive budget that includes both startup costs and these operational expenses to understand the total financial commitment required.

Don't forget about marketing and branding, which are essential for attracting customers. Developing a strong brand identity can involve costs like designing a logo, building a website, or creating promotional materials. Even if you're working with a limited budget, there are plenty of creative ways to market your business using social media or community events. Remember, every penny invested in effective marketing is a step forward in making your business a success.

Lastly, seek out resources and support available to young entrepreneurs. Many organizations and programs offer assistance, including grants, competitions, and workshops that can help reduce your startup costs. Discuss your plans with your parents or mentors, as they can provide valuable insights and possibly help you find additional funding sources. By understanding and planning for your startup costs, you set a solid foundation for your entrepreneurial journey, turning your innovative ideas into reality while navigating the exciting world of business.

Exploring Funding Options

Exploring funding options is a crucial step for young innovators eager to bring their business ideas to life. Whether you're thinking of launching a tech startup, a handcrafted goods shop, or a community service project, understanding where to find the necessary funds can set you on the path to success. There are several avenues to explore that can help you secure the financial backing needed to turn your vision into reality.

One of the most accessible options for young entrepreneurs is personal savings. Starting small by saving a portion of your allowance, birthday money, or earnings from part-time jobs can create a solid foundation for your business. This approach not only gives you the capital to invest in your idea but also instills a sense of responsibility and financial discipline. By managing your savings effectively, you can learn valuable lessons about budgeting and the importance of financial planning, which will serve you well in the future.

Another exciting avenue to consider is crowdfunding. Platforms like Kickstarter and Indiegogo allow you to present your idea to the public and raise funds by getting people excited about your project. This method not only provides the financial support you might need but also helps you build a community around your business concept. As you share your vision, you will engage with potential customers and supporters who can offer feedback, encouragement, and even help promote your project. Crowdfunding can transform your idea into a collaborative effort, making it feel more like a shared journey.

In addition to personal savings and crowdfunding, you might want to explore grants and competitions specifically designed for young entrepreneurs. Various organizations and foundations offer financial awards to help support innovative ideas and projects. Participating in these competitions can also provide valuable experience in pitching your business concept and refining your presentation skills. Even if you don't win, the application process can teach you how to articulate your vision and may open doors to mentorship opportunities or networking with other entrepreneurs.

Lastly, consider seeking support from family and friends. Often, those closest to you are willing to invest in your dreams, whether it's through small loans or gifts to help you get started. Be open and honest with them about your goals and how their support can make a difference. This approach not only provides you with funding but can also be a source of encouragement and motivation as you embark on your entrepreneurial journey. Remember, every great business starts with a single step, and exploring these funding options is an empowering way to take that step confidently.

Creating a Budget

Creating a budget is one of the most essential steps in starting your first business. It may seem daunting at first, but a budget is simply a plan that helps you manage your money wisely. By taking the time to outline your income and expenses, you can gain control over your finances and make informed decisions about your business. This process not only sets the foundation for your entrepreneurial journey but also empowers you to track your progress and achieve your goals.

To start, gather all the information you need about your potential income and expenses. Think about how much money you expect to make from your business, whether it's from sales, services, or any other revenue streams. Next, list all the costs associated with running your business. These might include materials, marketing, equipment, and any other necessary expenses. Remember, being thorough in this step will help you avoid surprises down the road, so take your time to think of everything you might need.

Once you have outlined your income and expenses, it's time to organize this information. Creating a simple spreadsheet or using budgeting software can help you visualize your financial situation. You can categorize your expenses into fixed costs, which remain the same each month, and variable costs, which can fluctuate. This clarity will enable you to see where your money is going and identify areas where you can cut back if needed. Having a clear view of your finances not only prepares you for challenges but can also reveal opportunities for growth.

As you create your budget, it's crucial to set financial goals. These goals can be short-term, like saving for a specific piece of equipment, or long-term, such as reaching a certain level of sales within a year. Setting achievable goals motivates you to stick to your budget and gives you a sense of purpose. Celebrate your milestones along the way, no matter how small they may seem. Each step forward is a victory that brings you closer to your dreams.

Finally, remember that your budget is a living document. As you progress in your business, your income and expenses will likely change. Review and adjust your budget regularly to reflect these changes. This adaptability is key to staying on track and ensuring that your business remains financially healthy. By embracing the budgeting process, you are not just managing your money; you are building a solid foundation for your entrepreneurial success. Keep pushing forward, and let your budget guide you on this exciting journey!

Chapter 5: Marketing Your Business

Defining Your Target Audience

Defining your target audience is a crucial step in launching a successful business. As a young innovator, you might wonder who will be most interested in what you offer. Taking the time to identify your ideal customers can make all the difference in your entrepreneurial journey. Start by considering the demographics of your potential audience, such as their age, gender, location, and interests. Understanding these characteristics will help you tailor your products or services to meet their specific needs, making your business more appealing and relevant.

Next, delve deeper into the psychographics of your audience. This involves exploring their values, beliefs, lifestyles, and behaviors. Consider what motivates them and what challenges they face. For instance, if you're developing a product aimed at fellow students, think about their daily routines, preferences in technology, and the types of social issues that resonate with them. By connecting with your audience on a personal level, you can create a brand that feels relatable and trustworthy, which can significantly enhance customer loyalty.

Don't forget to leverage the power of research when defining your target audience. Utilize surveys, interviews, and social media platforms to gather insights about your potential customers. Engaging with them directly allows you to understand their desires and pain points better. You can also analyze existing businesses in your niche to see who their audience is and identify any gaps in the market that your business could fill. This research will provide you with a solid foundation and inspire innovative ideas that resonate with your target demographic.

As you define your audience, remember that flexibility is key. The preferences and needs of your customers may evolve over time, especially in today's fast-paced world. Stay attuned to feedback from your audience and be willing to adapt your offerings accordingly. This responsiveness not only shows that you value their opinions, but it also positions your business as one that is in tune with its customers, enhancing your credibility and relevance in the market.

Lastly, involve your parents or mentors in this process. They can provide valuable insights and perspectives based on their experiences. Collaborating with them can help you refine your understanding of your target audience and strengthen your business strategy. Defining your target audience is not just about numbers; it's about building connections. With dedication and an open mind, you'll be well on your way to creating a business that speaks directly to the hearts and minds of your customers.

Crafting Your Brand Message

Crafting your brand message is a vital step in establishing a successful business. Your brand message communicates who you are, what you stand for, and why your product or service matters. For young innovators, this is an opportunity to express your unique perspective and passion. Start by reflecting on your values and the reasons behind your entrepreneurial journey. Consider what inspires you and what you want to change in the world. This self-discovery process will help you articulate a compelling brand message that resonates with your audience.

Once you have a clear understanding of your values, think about your target audience. Who are the people you want to reach with your brand? Understanding their needs, preferences, and challenges is essential to crafting a message that speaks directly to them. Engage in conversations, conduct surveys, or explore social media to gather insights. This research will allow you to tailor your brand message, making it relatable and relevant. Remember, your audience is more likely to connect with your brand if they feel understood and valued.

Next, focus on the emotional aspect of your brand message. What feelings do you want to evoke in your audience? Whether it's excitement, trust, or inspiration, your message should create a connection that goes beyond the transactional. Share your story and the journey that led you to launch your business. Authenticity is key; people appreciate honesty and vulnerability. By showcasing the challenges you've faced and the lessons you've learned, you not only build credibility but also inspire others to follow their dreams.

Incorporate your brand's personality into your message. Are you playful, serious, innovative, or approachable? Your tone and style should reflect the essence of your brand. Use language that resonates with your audience and aligns with your values. Consider using visuals, such as logos and color schemes, to reinforce your message. A consistent brand identity helps create recognition and loyalty among your audience. As you develop your brand message, think of it as a story that invites people in and encourages them to join your journey.

Lastly, test and refine your brand message. Share it with friends, family, or mentors and gather feedback. Be open to making adjustments based on their perspectives. This iterative process is crucial in ensuring that your message not only represents you but also resonates with your audience. As you navigate the world of entrepreneurship, remember that your brand message is an evolving narrative. Embrace the changes and stay true to your vision. With passion and persistence, your brand message will become a powerful tool in building a meaningful connection with your audience and achieving your entrepreneurial goals.

Utilizing Social Media

Social media is a powerful tool for young innovators looking to launch their first business. With billions of users worldwide, platforms like Instagram, Facebook, Twitter, and TikTok provide an unparalleled opportunity to connect with potential customers, showcase products, and build a brand.

As a young entrepreneur, leveraging these platforms effectively can set you apart from the competition. It's not just about posting; it's about creating engaging content that resonates with your audience and encourages them to take action.

One of the most effective ways to utilize social media is by telling your story. People connect with stories, especially those that are authentic and relatable. Share your journey as an entrepreneur, including your challenges, successes, and the lessons you've learned along the way. This transparency builds trust with your audience and makes them feel invested in your business. Encourage your followers to engage with your story by asking questions or sharing their experiences.

The more you interact, the stronger your community becomes.

Visual content is another key element when it comes to social media. High-quality images and videos can capture attention and convey your brand's message quickly. For adolescents, creativity is often at the forefront, so don't hesitate to showcase your unique perspective. Use platforms like Instagram and TikTok to create eye-catching visuals that highlight your products or services. Consider tutorials, behind-the-scenes looks, or even customer testimonials as ways to engage your audience and demonstrate your business's value.

Consistency is crucial in building a social media presence. Regularly posting content keeps your audience engaged and helps you stay top-of-mind. Create a content calendar to plan your posts and ensure a steady flow of information. Encourage your followers to interact with your posts by asking for their opinions or running polls. By making your audience feel involved, you foster loyalty and encourage them to spread the word about your business.

Lastly, remember that social media is not just about promotion; it's also about community. Follow other young entrepreneurs, engage with their content, and collaborate where possible. Networking online can lead to valuable partnerships and insights that can enhance your business. By supporting one another, you create a positive environment that inspires creativity and innovation. Embrace the power of social media as a young innovator, and watch your entrepreneurial dreams come to life.

Chapter 6: Developing Your Product or Service

Designing Your Offering

Designing your offering is one of the most exciting parts of starting your first business. This is where your ideas begin to take shape and become something tangible that you can share with the world. Think of your offering as the solution to a problem or a way to make life a little more enjoyable for your customers. Whether you're creating a product, a service, or a unique experience, the key is to focus on what makes your offering special and how it can benefit others. Embrace your creativity and let your passion guide you as you brainstorm ideas.

Start by identifying the needs and wants of your target audience. Who are the people you want to serve? What problems do they face that you can help solve? Conducting surveys, interviews, or simply having conversations with your peers can provide valuable insights. Don't be afraid to ask questions and gather feedback. This research will not only inform your design process but will also help you build a connection with your potential customers, making them feel valued and understood.

Once you have a clear understanding of your audience, it's time to brainstorm ideas for your offering. Consider different formats—could it be a physical product, a digital service, or an event? Write down all your ideas, no matter how wild they may seem. Remember, innovation often comes from thinking outside the box. You might find inspiration in your hobbies, your daily life, or even in the challenges you and your friends face. The more you explore, the more likely you are to discover a unique angle that sets your offering apart from the competition.

After you've settled on a few promising ideas, it's important to prototype your offering. This doesn't mean you need a fully developed product right away; instead, create a simple version that you can test and refine. If you're designing a product, sketch it out or build a model. For services, outline what the customer experience will look like. Share your prototype with friends, family, or potential customers and gather their feedback. This step is crucial, as it allows you to identify any areas for improvement and ensures that your offering truly resonates with those you aim to serve.

Finally, remember that designing your offering is an iterative process. Don't be disheartened if your first idea doesn't hit the mark. Use feedback to make adjustments, and keep refining until you feel confident in what you have created. The journey of entrepreneurship is filled with learning opportunities, and each adjustment you make brings you closer to a successful offering. Stay positive and keep pushing forward; your passion and dedication will shine through in the final product, making it all the more valuable to your customers.

Prototyping and Testing

Prototyping and testing are crucial steps in transforming your innovative ideas into a successful business. As a young innovator, the process of creating a prototype allows you to visualize your concept and understand how it functions in the real world. This stage is not just about bringing your idea to life; it's about experimenting and learning from the results.

Don't be afraid to let your imagination run wild. Your prototype doesn't have to be perfect or expensive; it can be a simple sketch, a digital model, or even a physical representation made from everyday materials. The key is to get your idea out of your head and into a tangible form.

Once you have your prototype, the next step is testing. This is where the magic happens. Testing your prototype helps you gather valuable feedback, which can guide you in refining your product. Invite friends, family, or potential customers to try out your prototype and observe their reactions. Ask them specific questions about what they like and what could be improved. This process not only helps you identify potential flaws but also uncovers features that resonate with your audience. Remember, constructive criticism is a tool for growth, so embrace it with an open mind.

As you move through the testing phase, it's important to keep a journal of your findings. Documenting your thoughts, feedback, and any adjustments you make will provide a roadmap for your business journey. This journal becomes an invaluable resource as you continue to iterate on your prototype. It's also a great way to track your progress and see how far you've come. Each entry is a testament to your creativity and determination, reinforcing the idea that innovation is a process of trial and error rather than a straight path to success.

Don't forget that prototyping and testing can be fun! Embrace the challenges and celebrate your small victories. Every tweak you make is a step closer to realizing your vision. Involving your friends or family in this process can turn it into a collaborative adventure. You might be surprised by the ideas they bring to the table or how their insights can enhance your prototype. This teamwork not only builds your product but also strengthens relationships, making the journey enjoyable and memorable.

Finally, remember that the goal of prototyping and testing is not just to create a product but to foster a mindset of innovation and resilience. Every successful entrepreneur has faced setbacks, but those who learn from their experiences and keep pushing forward are the ones who ultimately succeed. So, take pride in your efforts, stay curious, and be willing to adapt. Your journey as a young innovator is just beginning, and with each prototype and test, you're building the foundation for a future filled with potential and opportunity.

Gathering Feedback

Gathering feedback is a crucial step in the entrepreneurial journey, especially for young innovators eager to make their mark. When you create a new product or service, it's easy to become attached to your idea. However, the reality is that the best way to refine your concept is to hear from others. Feedback provides valuable insights that can help you understand what works, what doesn't, and how you can improve. Don't be afraid to put your ideas out there; the opinions of others can guide you toward success.

Start by reaching out to friends, family, and classmates. These individuals are often your first supporters and can provide honest opinions about your idea. They may see things you might have overlooked or suggest improvements that can enhance your project. Encourage them to be candid in their feedback. This initial round of input can help you identify strengths and weaknesses in your offering before you approach a broader audience. Remember, constructive criticism is not a personal attack; it's a stepping stone toward making your idea even better.

Once you've gathered feedback from those close to you, it's time to expand your circle. Consider conducting surveys or focus groups with potential customers who fit your target market. Use online tools or social media to reach a wider audience. When you ask for feedback, be specific about what you want to know. Are you curious about the design, functionality, or price point? Clear questions can lead to more useful responses. Embrace the diversity of opinions you'll receive; different perspectives can illuminate aspects of your business that you hadn't considered before.

Listening to feedback is just as important as gathering it. Approach each piece of input with an open mind, recognizing that not all feedback will align with your vision. Take the time to analyze the responses and look for common themes. If multiple people mention the same issue, it's likely worth addressing. However, if feedback is mixed, trust your instincts and decide which suggestions resonate with your goals. This process will not only strengthen your business but also help you develop resilience as an entrepreneur.

Finally, it's essential to show appreciation to those who provide feedback. Thanking your supporters fosters goodwill and encourages them to continue participating in your journey. You can also share updates on how their input has influenced your project. This transparency builds trust and opens the door for future interactions. Remember, gathering feedback is not a one-time task; it's an ongoing process that will accompany you throughout your entrepreneurial career. Embrace it wholeheartedly, and you'll find yourself better equipped to navigate the exciting challenges of building your first business.

Chapter 7: Legal Considerations

Choosing a Business Structure

Choosing the right business structure is a crucial step in your entrepreneurial journey. As a young innovator, understanding the various types of business structures can empower you to make informed decisions that align with your goals. Whether you're planning to run a small online store, a service-based business, or a creative venture, selecting the right framework will set the foundation for your success. So, let's dive into the available options and what they mean for you and your budding enterprise.

The most common business structures include sole proprietorships, partnerships, limited liability companies (LLCs), and corporations. A sole proprietorship is the simplest form; it allows you to own and operate your business independently. This means all decisions are yours to make, giving you complete creative control. However, keep in mind that with this autonomy comes personal liability for any debts or legal issues that arise. If you're ready to take on that responsibility, a sole proprietorship could be an excellent fit for your startup.

If you're thinking about teaming up with friends or family, a partnership could be the way to go. Partnerships allow you to share responsibilities, resources, and ideas with others, fostering a collaborative environment. This structure can be particularly beneficial for young innovators who might lack certain skills or resources. Just remember, with a partnership comes shared liability, so it's important to choose your partners wisely and establish clear agreements to avoid conflicts down the road.

For those looking for a bit more protection and flexibility, forming an LLC might be the best choice. An LLC combines the benefits of sole proprietorships and partnerships while providing personal liability protection. This means that your personal assets are generally safe from business debts and lawsuits, which can be a huge relief for young entrepreneurs. Additionally, an LLC offers the flexibility of managing the business without many of the formalities required by corporations, making it perfect for innovative minds who want to focus on creativity and growth.

Finally, if you have big dreams and plan to scale your business significantly, consider the corporate structure. Corporations can attract investors and raise capital more easily, which is essential for growth. However, they come with more regulations and tax obligations. This option might seem daunting, but if you have a vision for a large-scale impact, it can be worth it. Remember, each business structure has its pros and cons, so take your time to assess what aligns best with your vision, resources, and long-term goals. With the right structure in place, you'll be one step closer to turning your innovative ideas into a thriving business.

Registering Your Business

Registering your business is a crucial step that can set the foundation for your entrepreneurial journey. This process may seem daunting, especially for young innovators, but it's an essential part of turning your ideas into a legitimate venture. By officially registering your business, you gain credibility, protect your brand, and open doors to various opportunities, including funding and partnerships.

Remember, every successful entrepreneur started somewhere, and taking this step is a significant move toward realizing your dreams.

Before you dive into the registration process, it's essential to understand the different types of business structures available. Each structure—such as a sole proprietorship, partnership, limited liability company (LLC), or corporation—comes with its own legal implications, tax responsibilities, and levels of personal liability. As a young entrepreneur, you might find that a sole proprietorship or an LLC suits your needs best, offering simplicity and flexibility. Take some time to research these options, discuss them with your parents or guardians, and choose the one that aligns best with your business goals.

Once you've chosen a business structure, the next step is to choose an appealing name for your business. Your business name is your identity in the marketplace, so make it memorable and reflective of what you offer. After you've brainstormed some ideas, check to see if your desired name is available. This often involves conducting a search through your local business registry and ensuring that no one else is using the name. Securing a unique name not only helps you stand out but also avoids potential legal issues down the road. After you've selected your business name, it's time to handle the paperwork. This step might sound tedious, but think of it as a rite of passage in your entrepreneurial journey. You'll typically need to fill out registration forms, pay a fee, and possibly obtain any necessary licenses or permits specific to your industry. The requirements can vary greatly depending on where you live and what type of business you're starting, so it's wise to check with local government websites or consult with a mentor who has experience in business. Completing this process signifies that you're serious about your venture and ready to take on the challenges ahead.

Finally, don't forget to celebrate this achievement! Registering your business is a significant milestone that deserves recognition. Share the news with your friends and family—this is a moment to be proud of! You've taken substantial steps toward building something of your own, and that determination will serve you well as you navigate the challenges of entrepreneurship. Remember, every great business starts with a single step, and you've just taken a major one. Embrace the journey ahead, keep learning, and continue innovating!

Understanding Licenses and Permits

Understanding licenses and permits is an essential step for any young entrepreneur eager to bring their business ideas to life. As you embark on this exciting journey, it's important to grasp the basics of what licenses and permits are, why they matter, and how to obtain them. These legal requirements serve as a way to ensure that businesses operate safely, fairly, and in accordance with local regulations. While the process may seem daunting at first, remember that every successful entrepreneur navigates these waters, and you can too.

The first thing to know is that licenses and permits vary widely depending on the type of business you want to start and where you live. For example, if you're planning to run a lemonade stand, you might need a simple vendor's permit. However, if your entrepreneurial aspirations involve opening a tech startup or a food truck, you'll likely face more complex requirements. Researching local laws and regulations is crucial. Don't hesitate to ask for help from parents or guardians; they can guide you through the maze of requirements and help you understand what applies specifically to your venture.

Once you know what you need, the next step is the application process. This can involve filling out forms, paying fees, and sometimes even attending meetings or inspections. While this may sound like a lot of work, think of it as an opportunity to learn valuable skills like organization and perseverance. Each step you take is a building block toward your dream. Many young entrepreneurs find that the experience of applying for licenses and permits teaches them about accountability and responsibility—qualities that will serve them well in any future endeavor.

Don't let the prospect of legal requirements intimidate you. Instead, view them as a necessary part of your entrepreneurial journey. They are not just hurdles to jump over; they are a way of ensuring that you're operating your business ethically and legally. This foundation not only protects you but also builds trust with your customers. When they see that you have all the necessary permits, they'll feel more confident in doing business with you. This trust can lead to long-term relationships and a loyal customer base.

Finally, remember that understanding licenses and permits is just one aspect of running a successful business. It may seem like a small part of your overall journey, but it plays a vital role in setting you up for success. Embrace this process as a valuable learning experience, and don't hesitate to reach out for support. Whether it's through online resources, local business workshops, or advice from experienced entrepreneurs, there's a wealth of knowledge available to help you thrive. With determination and the right information, you can navigate the world of licenses and permits and focus on what truly matters—bringing your innovative ideas to life.

Chapter 8: Launching Your Business

Creating a Launch Plan

Creating a launch plan is a crucial step in transforming your innovative idea into a thriving business. It's like a roadmap that guides you through the exciting journey of entrepreneurship. As you embark on this adventure, remember that planning is not just a task; it's an opportunity to clarify your vision and set achievable goals. The process may seem daunting, but with a little creativity and determination, you can create a plan that reflects your aspirations and paves the way for success.

Start by defining your business goals. What do you want to achieve in the short term and the long term? Setting specific, measurable, achievable, relevant, and time-bound (SMART) goals can help you stay focused. For instance, you might aim to launch your product within six months or reach a particular number of customers by the end of the first year. Writing down these goals not only solidifies your intentions but also serves as a motivational tool to keep you on track as you navigate the ups and downs of entrepreneurship.

Next, identify your target market. Who are your ideal customers, and what problems does your product or service solve for them? Conducting some market research can provide valuable insights into your audience's preferences and behaviors. Engaging with potential customers through surveys, interviews, or social media can help you refine your approach. Understanding your target market will not only help you tailor your offerings but also ensure that your marketing efforts resonate with the right people.

Once you have a clear understanding of your goals and audience, it's time to develop your marketing strategy. Think about how you will promote your business and attract customers. Will you use social media, local events, or word-of-mouth to spread the word? Consider creating a budget for marketing activities and allocate resources accordingly. Being creative in your approach can set you apart from competitors and help you build a loyal customer base. Remember, marketing is about storytelling; share your passion and the journey behind your business.

Finally, don't forget to establish a timeline for your launch plan. Break down your goals into actionable steps and assign deadlines to each task. This timeline will help you stay organized and accountable as you work towards your launch. Celebrate small victories along the way, as they will keep your spirits high and motivate you to push forward. With determination and a well-thought-out launch plan, you'll be well-prepared to share your innovative ideas with the world and embark on a successful entrepreneurial journey.

Building Excitement

Building excitement is a crucial element in the journey of young innovators embarking on their entrepreneurial adventures. When you first conceive an idea, that spark of inspiration can ignite a powerful motivation within you. This initial enthusiasm is not just a fleeting feeling; it can be the foundation upon which you build your business. Embrace that excitement! It fuels creativity and encourages you to explore new possibilities. Share your vision with friends and family; their encouragement can amplify your energy and help you refine your ideas further.

As you start to develop your business concept, it's important to keep that excitement alive. One effective way to do this is by setting small, achievable goals. Celebrate each milestone you reach, no matter how minor it may seem. Whether it's creating a logo, finalizing a product, or even securing your first customer, each step is a victory. These celebrations not only boost your morale but also keep you motivated to push forward. Remember, every great business was built one small step at a time.

Engaging with your community can also build excitement around your venture. Consider hosting a small event or workshop to showcase your idea. This not only introduces your concept to potential customers but also allows you to connect with other young innovators who share your passion. The energy created in these interactions can be contagious, inspiring not just you but also your peers. Networking in this way can open doors to new opportunities and partnerships that you may not have envisioned before.

In addition, leverage social media to share your journey. Documenting your progress can create a sense of accountability while also allowing others to follow along. By sharing your highs and lows, you invite your audience into your entrepreneurial world, fostering a community of supporters. When people see your passion and determination, they are more likely to rally behind you. It's a powerful way to generate excitement not just for your business, but for the entrepreneurial spirit as a whole.

Finally, don't underestimate the power of mentorship. Seek out individuals who have experience in your field or who have successfully started their own businesses. Their insights can not only help you refine your ideas but also inspire you to dream bigger. A mentor can provide encouragement during challenging times, reminding you of the excitement that sparked your journey in the first place. By surrounding yourself with positivity and support, you create an environment where excitement can thrive, setting the stage for your success as a young innovator.

Hosting a Launch Event

Hosting a launch event is an exciting opportunity for young innovators to showcase their hard work and bring their business ideas to life. This event serves as a platform to introduce your product or service to the world, attract potential customers, and create buzz around your brand. Planning a successful launch requires creativity, organization, and a clear understanding of your target audience. With the right approach, your launch event can set the stage for your entrepreneurial journey.

First, consider the venue for your launch event. It could be a local community center, a park, or even your own backyard. The key is to select a space that reflects the spirit of your business and is accessible to your audience. As you plan, think about the atmosphere you want to create. Will it be casual and fun, or more formal and professional? Your choice of venue will influence the overall vibe of the event, so choose a place that resonates with your brand identity and appeals to your target market.

Next, marketing your event is crucial to building excitement and ensuring a good turnout. Utilize social media platforms where your peers are active, such as Instagram, TikTok, or Snapchat, to promote your event. Create eye-catching graphics, share sneak peeks of what attendees can expect, and encourage your friends and family to spread the word. Additionally, consider reaching out to local influencers or community groups who might be interested in your product or service. With effective marketing, you can generate buzz and attract an audience eager to support your venture.

During the event, engage your guests with interactive activities. Set up stations where attendees can try out your product, participate in fun contests, or provide feedback on your business idea. This not only makes the event more enjoyable but also helps you gather valuable insights and build relationships with potential customers. Don't forget to create a welcoming atmosphere by providing refreshments and ensuring that your guests feel appreciated. A well-hosted event can leave a lasting impression, turning attendees into loyal supporters of your brand.

Finally, after the event, take time to reflect on the experience. Gather feedback from participants to understand what worked well and what could be improved for future events. Celebrate your achievements, no matter how big or small, and use this momentum to propel your business forward.

Hosting a launch event is not just about the immediate success; it's about building connections, learning from the experience, and establishing a foundation for your entrepreneurial journey. Embrace this opportunity, and let your passion shine through as you take your first steps in the world of business.

Chapter 9: Managing Your Business

Basic Financial Management

Basic financial management is a crucial skill for any young innovator embarking on their entrepreneurial journey. Understanding how to handle money effectively can set the foundation for a successful business and promote responsible financial habits. By grasping the essentials of budgeting, saving, and investing, adolescents can make informed decisions that will benefit their ventures and personal finances for years to come.

To begin, creating a budget is one of the first steps in financial management. A budget is a simple plan that outlines expected income and expenses over a specific period. For young entrepreneurs, this means tracking any money earned from their business activities, alongside any personal allowances or gifts. By categorizing expenses, such as materials needed for projects or promotional costs, they can visualize where their funds are going. This not only helps in managing current finances but also teaches the importance of financial discipline and foresight.

Saving is another key element of financial management. Young innovators should aim to save a portion of their earnings, whether it's for reinvesting in their business or for personal goals. Setting a savings goal can provide motivation and a sense of accomplishment. It can be as simple as aiming to save a certain percentage of every dollar earned. This habit not only prepares them for future investments but also instills a sense of security and responsibility in managing their finances.

Investing is the next step that can help young entrepreneurs grow their wealth over time. While it might seem daunting at first, understanding the basics of investing can open up new opportunities. Adolescents can start small, perhaps by learning about stocks, bonds, or even peer-to-peer lending. By researching and making informed decisions, they can see how their money can work for them. This experience can also teach valuable lessons about risk, reward, and the importance of patience in achieving financial goals.

Finally, seeking guidance from parents, mentors, or financial resources can enhance financial literacy. Engaging in discussions about money management can demystify complex concepts and provide practical insights. Encouraging open dialogue about financial decisions fosters a supportive environment for learning. By embracing these basic financial management principles, young innovators not only equip themselves with essential skills for their entrepreneurial endeavors but also lay the groundwork for a financially sound future.

Time Management Tips

Time management is a crucial skill for young innovators who are venturing into the world of entrepreneurship. Balancing schoolwork, personal interests, and the demands of a budding business can feel overwhelming. However, with a few effective strategies, you can maximize your productivity and find greater satisfaction in all your endeavors. Start by setting clear goals. Establish both short-term and long-term objectives for your business and personal life. Write them down and keep them visible so you can regularly assess your progress. This clarity will help you prioritize your tasks and stay focused on what truly matters.

Creating a structured schedule can be a game-changer. Use a planner or digital calendar to map out your week, allocating specific time blocks for school, work, and relaxation. Be sure to include breaks to recharge your mind and prevent burnout.

Sticking to a routine can significantly enhance your efficiency. Remember to stay flexible; life can be unpredictable, and adjusting your plans is part of the process. By developing this habit, you'll find it easier to manage your time effectively while still enjoying the freedom of being a teenager.

Another valuable tip is to break tasks into smaller, manageable chunks. Instead of feeling daunted by a large project, divide it into specific steps that can be completed one at a time. This approach not only reduces anxiety but also provides a sense of accomplishment as you tick off each task. For instance, if you're launching a website for your business, you might set aside time for research, design, and content creation separately. Celebrating these small victories can motivate you to keep pushing forward.

In addition to planning and breaking tasks down, it's essential to eliminate distractions. Identify what typically pulls your attention away from your work. It might be social media, TV, or even chatting with friends. Create a workspace that minimizes these distractions, and set boundaries for when you'll engage in leisure activities. By dedicating uninterrupted time to your tasks, you'll find yourself completing them more quickly and efficiently, leaving more time for relaxation and enjoyment.

Lastly, don't hesitate to seek support. Whether it's from parents, teachers, or friends, sharing your challenges and successes can provide valuable insights and encouragement. Surrounding yourself with a supportive network can make a significant difference in your ability to manage time effectively. Remember, entrepreneurship is a journey, and learning to manage your time is an essential skill that will serve you well throughout your life. Embrace the process, stay organized, and you'll be well on your way to achieving your goals.

Building a Support Network

Building a support network is a crucial step in your entrepreneurial journey. As you embark on the exciting path of starting your own business, having a group of people who understand, encourage, and assist you can make all the difference. This network can consist of friends, family, mentors, and fellow entrepreneurs who can provide guidance, share experiences, and help you navigate the challenges of entrepreneurship. Surrounding yourself with supportive individuals not only boosts your confidence but also fosters an environment where you can thrive creatively and strategically.

Start by reaching out to those closest to you. Family and friends often want to see you succeed and can offer valuable perspectives. Share your business ideas with them and ask for their input. They may have insights you hadn't considered or connections that could be beneficial. Engaging with your immediate circle creates a foundation of support, and this encouragement can motivate you during challenging times. It's essential to communicate openly about your ambitions and listen to their thoughts, as this dialogue can strengthen your relationships and provide you with diverse viewpoints.

Next, consider seeking out mentors who have experience in your area of interest. A mentor can be a teacher, a family friend, or a local business owner who is willing to share their knowledge. They can provide you with practical advice, help you avoid common pitfalls, and inspire you with their own success stories. Look for networking events or workshops in your community where you can meet potential mentors. Building these relationships takes time, but the insights and support you gain can be invaluable as you navigate the complexities of starting a business.

In addition to family and mentors, connect with other young entrepreneurs. Joining clubs, online forums, or local entrepreneurship groups can introduce you to peers who are on similar journeys. These connections can lead to collaborations, sharing of resources, and even friendships that last a lifetime. Engaging with others who share your passion can also spark creativity and motivate you to push through obstacles. Remember, entrepreneurship can be a rollercoaster ride, and having friends who understand the ups and downs can make the journey much more enjoyable.

Finally, don't underestimate the power of online communities. Platforms like social media, forums, and entrepreneurial websites can provide access to a vast network of individuals who are eager to share their knowledge and experiences. Engage with these communities by asking questions, sharing your progress, and offering support to others. Building a supportive network, both in-person and online, creates a rich tapestry of resources that empowers you to pursue your entrepreneurial dreams with confidence and resilience. Embrace this opportunity to connect, learn, and grow alongside others who are just as passionate about innovation and success as you are.

Chapter 10: Learning from Experience

Embracing Failure

Failure is often seen as a roadblock, something to avoid at all costs. However, in the world of entrepreneurship, failure can be one of the most powerful teachers. For young innovators, understanding that failure is not the end, but rather a stepping stone toward success, is essential. Embracing failure means recognizing it as an integral part of the learning process. Each setback presents an opportunity to analyze what went wrong, adjust your strategy, and try again with newfound knowledge. This mindset can transform the way you approach challenges in your business journey.

When you set out to create something new, whether it's a product, service, or even a creative project, the path will not always be smooth. There will be moments of doubt, mistakes made, and ideas that don't pan out as expected. Instead of viewing these moments as personal shortcomings, it's crucial to reframe them as valuable experiences. Many successful entrepreneurs have faced numerous failures before achieving their goals. Their stories serve as a reminder that perseverance and a willingness to learn from mistakes are key components of innovation.

Parents play a vital role in helping adolescent entrepreneurs navigate failure. Encouraging a growth mindset can empower young innovators to take risks without the fear of judgment. When parents model resilience and show that they too have faced setbacks in their own lives, it sets a powerful example. Open discussions about failure can help demystify the experience and reinforce the idea that every entrepreneur has faced challenges. This supportive environment allows adolescents to experiment, learn, and ultimately thrive in their entrepreneurial endeavors.

In addition to fostering resilience, embracing failure can enhance creativity. When young innovators are not afraid to fail, they are more likely to think outside the box and pursue unconventional ideas. This spirit of exploration can lead to breakthroughs that might not have been discovered otherwise. Encouraging experimentation, even if it leads to failure, can spark innovation and open up new avenues for success. Each attempt, whether it succeeds or fails, contributes to a deeper understanding of the market and the needs of potential customers.

Ultimately, embracing failure is about cultivating a positive attitude toward challenges. It teaches young innovators to be adaptable, to reassess their strategies, and to persist even when the going gets tough. By changing the narrative around failure from one of fear to one of opportunity, adolescents can approach entrepreneurship with confidence and resilience. With the right mindset, every failure becomes a lesson learned, paving the way for future successes and innovations.

Celebrating Successes

Celebrating successes is a crucial part of the entrepreneurial journey, especially for young innovators who are just beginning to navigate the world of business. Every small victory, whether it's landing your first customer, completing a project, or receiving positive feedback, deserves recognition. These moments not only boost your confidence but also reinforce the idea that your hard work is paying off. By taking the time to acknowledge and celebrate these milestones, you create a positive cycle that motivates you to push forward.

When you achieve a goal, no matter how minor it may seem, it is essential to pause and reflect on what you've accomplished. This reflection helps you understand the steps that led to your success and the skills you developed along the way. It's an opportunity to recognize the effort you put in, the lessons learned, and the support you received from friends and family. Keeping a success journal can be a great way to document these achievements, serving as a tangible reminder of your progress that you can look back on when challenges arise.

Involving others in your celebrations can amplify the joy of your accomplishments. Share your successes with family, friends, and mentors who have been part of your journey. Their encouragement and pride in your achievements can provide a significant boost to your motivation. Organizing small celebrations, whether it's a gathering, a special dinner, or simply sharing the news on social media, helps build a supportive community around your entrepreneurial endeavors. Remember, you are not just celebrating your success; you are inspiring others to believe in their own potential.

Celebrating successes also helps to build resilience. Entrepreneurship is filled with ups and downs, and it's easy to become discouraged during tough times. By regularly celebrating your achievements, you create a reservoir of positive experiences to draw upon during challenging moments. These celebrations remind you of your capabilities and the progress you've made, reinforcing the belief that you can overcome obstacles and continue to innovate. This mindset is crucial for long-term success in business and personal growth.

Finally, it's important to set new goals after celebrating your successes. Each achievement opens the door to new possibilities and challenges. Use the momentum from your celebrations to propel yourself forward into the next phase of your entrepreneurial journey. Embrace the excitement of what lies ahead and keep pushing your boundaries. By consistently celebrating your successes and setting new goals, you create a dynamic cycle of growth that keeps your entrepreneurial spirit alive and thriving.

Continuous Improvement

Continuous improvement is a vital concept for any young entrepreneur looking to establish a successful business. It involves an ongoing effort to enhance products, services, or processes. By adopting a mindset of continuous improvement, young innovators can stay ahead of the competition and adapt to the ever-changing market landscape. This approach encourages you to regularly evaluate what you're doing, seek feedback, and implement small changes that can lead to significant advancements over time. Remember, every great business started as an idea that evolved through learning and growth.

One of the most effective ways to foster continuous improvement is by embracing a culture of feedback. As a young entrepreneur, it's essential to create an environment where you and your team feel comfortable sharing thoughts and suggestions. Encourage open communication and actively seek input from customers, mentors, and peers. This feedback can provide valuable insights into what's working well and what needs adjustment. Consider setting up regular brainstorming sessions or surveys to gather diverse perspectives. The more you listen, the more opportunities you'll have to refine your business practices.

Another crucial aspect of continuous improvement is setting measurable goals. Goals give you direction and a way to track your progress. Start by defining specific, achievable objectives for your business, whether it's increasing sales, enhancing customer satisfaction, or expanding your product line. Break these goals down into smaller, manageable tasks and regularly assess your progress. Celebrate your achievements, no matter how small, and use any setbacks as learning experiences. This process not only helps you stay motivated but also instills a sense of accomplishment as you witness your growth over time.

Incorporating technology and innovation into your continuous improvement efforts can lead to exciting advancements. Explore new tools and platforms that can streamline your processes, enhance productivity, or improve customer engagement. Stay updated on industry trends and be willing to experiment with new ideas. By embracing change and being open to trying new approaches, you'll position your business for success. Remember, innovation doesn't always mean drastic changes; sometimes, it's about finding smarter ways to do what you're already doing.

Lastly, instilling a lifelong learning mindset is essential for continuous improvement. Strive to expand your knowledge and skills regularly through workshops, online courses, and networking opportunities. Surround yourself with mentors who can guide you and share their experiences. The more you learn, the better equipped you'll be to navigate challenges and seize opportunities. Continuous improvement is not just a business strategy; it's a way of life. Embrace the journey, stay curious, and watch your entrepreneurial dreams flourish as you commit to constant growth and development.

Chapter 11: Inspiring Stories of Young Innovators

Case Studies of Successful Young Entrepreneurs

In the world of entrepreneurship, age is often just a number, and the stories of young entrepreneurs demonstrate that determination, creativity, and hard work can lead to remarkable success. One notable case is that of Moziah Bridges, who started his bow tie business, Mo's Bows, at the tender age of nine. Inspired by his love for fashion and the desire to dress well, Moziah began sewing bow ties from his grandmother's kitchen. His passion quickly blossomed into a thriving business, attracting national attention and even a deal on the television show Shark Tank. Moziah's journey illustrates that with a clear vision and relentless pursuit, even a young person can make a significant impact in the business world.

Another inspiring example is Mikaila Ulmer, who launched her lemonade company, Me & the Bees Lemonade, when she was just four years old. After being stung by bees and learning about their dwindling population, Mikaila decided to create a lemonade recipe using honey instead of sugar. Her entrepreneurial spirit led her to sell her product at local events, and soon she was able to secure a deal with major retailers. Mikaila's commitment to sustainability and her passion for saving bees show that young entrepreneurs can not only succeed in business but also contribute positively to the world around them.

Cory Nieves, known as "Mr. Cory," began his venture at just six years old when he started a cookie business to help his mother buy a car. What began as a simple effort to make a difference in his family's life turned into a successful brand. Today, Mr. Cory's Cookies is a recognized name, and Cory has become a role model for young entrepreneurs everywhere. His story emphasizes the importance of setting goals and working diligently to achieve them, no matter how small the initial steps may seem. Young people can learn from Cory that passion combined with purpose can lead to extraordinary achievements.

Another remarkable young entrepreneur is Ben Pasternak, who created a social media app called Flogg at the age of 15. His application garnered millions of downloads, leading to lucrative opportunities in the tech industry. Ben's journey highlights the importance of harnessing technological advancements and trends to create innovative solutions. For adolescents interested in entrepreneurship, Ben's story serves as a reminder that creativity and technical skills can open doors to exciting possibilities, encouraging them to explore their interests and leverage their unique talents.

These case studies of successful young entrepreneurs not only inspire but also provide valuable lessons for adolescents and their parents. Each story showcases the power of resilience, creativity, and the willingness to learn from failures. As young innovators embark on their entrepreneurial journeys, they should remember that age does not define capability. With passion, guidance, and a strong support system, any young person can transform their ideas into thriving businesses. By believing in themselves and embracing their entrepreneurial spirit, they can follow in the footsteps of these remarkable young leaders and forge their own paths to success.

Lessons Learned from Their Journeys

Lessons learned from the journeys of young innovators can serve as invaluable guidance for aspiring entrepreneurs. Each story is unique, filled with challenges and triumphs that provide insights into what it takes to start and sustain a business. One common lesson is the importance of resilience. Many young entrepreneurs faced setbacks that tested their determination. Instead of giving up, they learned to adapt and pivot their ideas, which ultimately led to greater success.

This resilience not only builds character but also equips them with the skills to tackle future obstacles with confidence.

Another significant lesson is the power of collaboration. Young innovators often realized that they did not have to navigate their entrepreneurial journeys alone. By seeking out mentors, forming partnerships, and building networks, they gained diverse perspectives that enriched their ideas and strategies. Collaboration fosters creativity and can lead to unexpected opportunities. For adolescents considering entrepreneurship, understanding the value of teamwork early on can set the foundation for future ventures and help them cultivate relationships that may benefit them throughout their careers.

Additionally, the experiences of young innovators highlight the necessity of continuous learning. Many entrepreneurs discovered that their initial assumptions about business were often incorrect. They learned to embrace feedback and criticism, viewing them as opportunities for growth rather than as setbacks. This open-mindedness allowed them to refine their products, understand their customers better, and adapt to market demands. Cultivating a mindset of lifelong learning is essential for young entrepreneurs, as it prepares them to adapt in an ever-changing business landscape.

Time management emerged as another critical lesson. Young innovators quickly realized that balancing school, personal life, and their business required diligent planning and prioritization. Developing effective time management skills enabled them to work more efficiently and maintain their commitments. They learned to set clear goals and break tasks into manageable parts, which not only kept them organized but also reduced stress. Adolescents can take these lessons to heart, as mastering time management early on can lead to greater success in all areas of life.

Lastly, the journeys of young innovators teach us about the importance of belief in one's vision. Many faced skepticism from peers and adults alike, but their passion and conviction drove them to pursue their ideas relentlessly. This unwavering belief in themselves and their visions fueled their motivation and inspired others to support them. For aspiring entrepreneurs, understanding that self-belief is crucial can empower them to chase their dreams without fear of judgment. Embracing these lessons can create a strong foundation for young innovators as they embark on their entrepreneurial journeys, equipping them with the tools and mindset needed for success.

How They Overcame Challenges

Young innovators often face a multitude of challenges on their entrepreneurial journey, but overcoming these obstacles is not only possible, it can also be a powerful learning experience. Many successful young entrepreneurs have encountered setbacks that seemed insurmountable at first. However, by embracing these hurdles, they cultivated resilience and creativity, which ultimately helped them thrive. The key is to view challenges as valuable opportunities for growth rather than as roadblocks.

One common challenge faced by young entrepreneurs is a lack of experience. Many adolescents feel intimidated by their limited knowledge and skills in business. However, numerous innovators have turned this perceived weakness into an advantage. They sought mentorship, attended workshops, and engaged in online courses to build their understanding of entrepreneurship. By actively seeking resources and guidance, they not only gained confidence but also equipped themselves with the tools necessary to navigate the complexities of running a business.

Another significant hurdle is the fear of failure. Young innovators often worry about making mistakes or not meeting expectations. This fear can be paralyzing, preventing them from taking the first step. However, many successful entrepreneurs have shared their stories of initial failures and the lessons learned from them. They discovered that failure is not the end but rather a stepping stone to success. By reframing their mindset and embracing risk, they found the courage to pursue their ideas and learned invaluable lessons that shaped their future endeavors.

Time management is another challenge that young entrepreneurs frequently encounter. Balancing school, extracurricular activities, and personal life with the demands of a budding business can feel overwhelming. However, many innovators have developed effective strategies to manage their time. By creating structured schedules, prioritizing tasks, and setting realistic goals, they found ways to maintain a healthy balance. This not only improved their productivity but also taught them essential life skills that would benefit them in all areas of their lives.

Finally, financial constraints can pose a significant barrier to launching a business. Young innovators often struggle with limited funds and resources, which can be discouraging. Yet, many have found creative solutions to this challenge by exploring alternative funding options such as crowdfunding, grants, or small loans. They learned to budget wisely and seek partnerships that could provide support. By approaching their financial limitations with innovation and determination, they not only overcame these obstacles but also gained a deeper understanding of financial literacy, which is crucial for any entrepreneur.

Chapter 12: The Future of Your Business

Setting Long-Term Goals

Setting long-term goals is a vital step in the journey of young innovators. These goals serve as a roadmap, guiding your decisions and actions as you navigate the exciting world of entrepreneurship. When you take the time to outline what you want to achieve in the future, you create a vision that inspires you to take the necessary steps today. Long-term goals can help you stay focused, measure your progress, and maintain motivation, even when challenges arise.

The first step in setting long-term goals is to reflect on your passions and interests. What excites you? What problems do you want to solve? By identifying what truly matters to you, you can create goals that resonate with your personal values and aspirations. This alignment will not only make the journey more enjoyable but also increase your commitment to seeing your goals through. Encourage open discussions with your parents or mentors about your ideas, as their insights can provide valuable perspectives.

Once you have a clear understanding of your passions, it's time to think big. Long-term goals should stretch your imagination and encourage you to envision the future you desire. Rather than setting limits based on your current circumstances, allow yourself to dream. Whether it's launching a groundbreaking app, starting a community service project, or inventing a new product, aim high. Writing these goals down can help solidify your commitment and serve as a constant reminder of what you're working towards.

As you set these ambitious goals, it's essential to break them down into manageable milestones. This approach not only makes the journey less overwhelming but also allows you to celebrate small victories along the way. For instance, if your long-term goal is to start your own business, consider what steps you need to take. This could include conducting market research, developing a business plan, or seeking out mentorship. Each milestone you achieve will build your confidence and keep you motivated to continue pushing forward.

Remember, setting long-term goals is not a one-time activity; it's an ongoing process. As you grow and evolve, so too may your goals and aspirations. Regularly revisiting and adjusting your goals will keep you aligned with your passions and the changing landscape of entrepreneurship. Embrace the journey, knowing that every step you take brings you closer to realizing your dreams. With determination and a clear vision, you have the power to shape your future and make a meaningful impact.

Adapting to Change

In the world of entrepreneurship, change is not just a possibility; it is a certainty. As young innovators, you will encounter shifting trends, evolving consumer preferences, and unexpected challenges. Adapting to change is a vital skill that can set you apart from others. Embracing change with an open mind allows you to discover new opportunities and find creative solutions. Remember, every successful entrepreneur has faced change and adapted to it, turning potential setbacks into stepping stones for growth.

One of the most powerful ways to adapt to change is by developing a mindset of flexibility. This means being willing to adjust your plans and strategies as needed. For instance, if you realize that your original business idea isn't resonating with your audience, rather than feeling discouraged, see it as a chance to pivot. Ask yourself what your customers truly need and how you can provide it. By being open to feedback and willing to experiment, you can refine your approach and create a product or service that genuinely meets the demands of the market.

Moreover, staying informed about industry trends and technological advancements can significantly enhance your adaptability. Regularly read articles, listen to podcasts, and engage with online communities related to your niche. By understanding what is happening in your field, you will be better positioned to anticipate changes and respond proactively. This knowledge not only helps you stay relevant but also empowers you to innovate and differentiate your business in a crowded market.

Collaboration is another essential aspect of adapting to change. Surround yourself with a diverse group of peers who can offer different perspectives and ideas. Whether it's through networking events, online forums, or school clubs, engaging with others can help you discover new approaches and solutions to challenges. Don't hesitate to seek mentorship from experienced entrepreneurs who can provide guidance and support as you navigate the ups and downs of your entrepreneurial journey.

Finally, cultivate resilience within yourself. Change can be stressful, and setbacks are an inevitable part of any entrepreneurial venture. Learning to bounce back from difficulties will not only make you a stronger innovator but also instill confidence in your abilities. Embrace challenges as opportunities for growth and remember that each experience contributes to your development as an entrepreneur. With resilience, flexibility, and a willingness to learn, you will not only adapt to change but thrive in it, paving the way for a successful business journey.

The Importance of Lifelong Learning

Lifelong learning is more than just a phrase; it's a mindset that can significantly impact your journey as an entrepreneur. In today's rapidly changing world, the ability to adapt and grow is essential. As technology evolves and industries transform, the skills you possess today may not suffice tomorrow. Embracing lifelong learning means committing to continuous development, allowing you to stay ahead of the curve and seize new opportunities. This proactive approach not only enhances your expertise but also builds resilience, ensuring you can navigate the challenges of starting and running a business.

For young innovators, the benefits of lifelong learning are immense. Engaging in various learning experiences—whether through formal education, online courses, workshops, or even self-directed study—fosters creativity and critical thinking. These qualities are vital for entrepreneurs, as they enable you to devise innovative solutions to problems, identify market gaps, and develop unique products or services. By constantly seeking knowledge, you are effectively training your mind to think outside the box, which is a crucial skill in the entrepreneurial landscape.

Moreover, lifelong learning enhances your ability to network and collaborate with others. As you venture into new areas of knowledge, you meet people from diverse backgrounds with different perspectives. These interactions can lead to partnerships, mentorship opportunities, and friendships that enrich your entrepreneurial journey. By surrounding yourself with a community of learners, you create a support system that encourages growth and inspires you to push your boundaries. Remember, entrepreneurship is not a solo journey; it thrives on collaboration and shared experiences. Parents play a pivotal role in fostering a culture of lifelong learning among their children. Encouraging curiosity, exploration, and a love for learning can significantly influence a young person's entrepreneurial mindset. Parents can model lifelong learning by pursuing their interests, sharing new discoveries, and discussing the importance of adaptability in a changing world. By creating an environment that values education and personal growth, you empower your children to embrace challenges and seek knowledge actively, setting them on a path to success.

In conclusion, adopting a lifelong learning approach is essential for any aspiring entrepreneur. It not only equips you with the skills necessary to thrive in a competitive landscape but also instills a sense of curiosity and adaptability that will serve you well throughout your career. So, whether you're exploring new technologies, attending workshops, or simply reading about the latest trends in your field, remember that every bit of knowledge gained is a stepping stone towards achieving your dreams. Embrace the journey of learning and watch as it transforms your entrepreneurial aspirations into reality.

May I ask you for a small favor?

At the outset, I want to give you big thanks for taking out time to read this book.

You could have chosen any other book, but you took mine, and I appreciate this.

I hope you got at least a few actionable insights that will have a positive impact on your day-to-day life.

Can I ask for 30 seconds more of your time?

I'd love it if you could leave a review about the book.

Reviews may not matter to big-name authors, but they're a tremendous help for authors like me, who don't have much following.

They help me to grow my readership by encouraging folks to take a chance on my books.

To put it straight, reviews are the lifeblood of any author.

Please leave your review by scanning the below QR code; it will directly lead you to the book review page.

It will just take less than a minute of your time, but will tremendously help me to reach out to more people, so please leave your review.

Thanks for your support of my work.

And I'd love to see your review on my page.

Book Summary

Embracing the Entrepreneurial Spirit

- Entrepreneurship empowers individuals to solve problems, take risks, and turn ideas into impactful realities.
- Creativity fuels innovation, helping entrepreneurs develop unique solutions and stand out in competitive markets.
- Discovering and aligning with personal passions is crucial for creating meaningful and sustainable ventures.

Finding Your Business Idea

- Identifying unmet market needs helps entrepreneurs create solutions that fill gaps and add value.
- Generating ideas through brainstorming, collaboration, and creative techniques unlocks innovative possibilities.
- Validating ideas through feedback, surveys, and prototypes ensures they resonate with real-world demands.

Building a Business Plan

- A business plan outlines the goals, strategies, and actions needed to transform ideas into successful businesses.
- Including market analysis, operational details, and financial projections provides a clear direction for growth.
- Setting specific goals and celebrating milestones maintains motivation and tracks progress effectively.

Funding Your Venture

- Understanding startup costs helps entrepreneurs plan for initial investments and ongoing expenses.
- Exploring funding sources like savings, crowdfunding, and grants makes financing more accessible.
- Developing a budget ensures responsible financial management and supports business sustainability.

Marketing Your Business

- Defining a target audience ensures offerings meet customer needs and preferences effectively.

- Crafting a compelling brand message builds trust and creates an emotional connection with customers.
- Utilizing social media amplifies outreach, fosters engagement, and strengthens brand visibility.

Developing Your Product or Service

- Designing offerings that address customer needs and solve problems is essential for success.
- Prototyping and testing ideas refine products and services based on user feedback and practical insights.
- Gathering feedback from diverse sources enhances innovation and improves the final product.

Legal Considerations

- Selecting the right business structure affects liability, taxation, and operational flexibility.
- Registering a business ensures legitimacy, protects branding, and fosters credibility.
- Complying with licensing and permitting requirements builds a trustworthy and lawful foundation.

Launching Your Business

- Creating a launch plan with SMART goals and market strategies ensures a focused and impactful start.
- Generating excitement through promotions, storytelling, and engagement builds anticipation and loyalty.
- Hosting a launch event provides an opportunity to showcase offerings and connect with potential customers.

Managing Your Business

- Financial management, including budgeting and saving, supports stability and long-term growth.
- Effective time management through prioritization and planning enhances productivity and work-life balance.
- Building a support network of mentors, peers, and family fosters guidance and shared success.

Learning from Experience

- Embracing failure as a learning opportunity builds resilience and fosters personal and professional growth.
- Celebrating successes boosts morale, recognizes progress, and motivates continued effort.
- Continuous improvement through feedback, innovation, and adaptation is essential for sustained success.

Inspiring Stories of Young Innovators

- Success stories of young entrepreneurs illustrate the power of creativity, perseverance, and innovation.
- Learning from others' journeys highlights strategies for overcoming challenges and achieving goals.
- Challenges inspire problem-solving, adaptability, and growth, shaping future success.

The Future of Your Business

- Adaptability is crucial for long-term success; businesses must embrace change and innovate continuously to stay relevant.

- Planning for growth involves setting clear goals, exploring new markets, and leveraging emerging technologies.
- Building a sustainable business requires balancing profitability with social responsibility and environmental impact.
- Developing leadership skills and fostering a strong company culture ensures resilience and a unified vision for the future.
- Continuous learning and staying informed about industry trends empower businesses to anticipate and navigate challenges effectively.

Acknowledgment

Creating *IGNITE-INNOVATE-LEAD* has been an extraordinary journey, and I am deeply grateful to everyone who played a part in making this book a reality.

First and foremost, my heartfelt thanks go to the young dreamers and aspiring entrepreneurs who inspired this book. Your passion, curiosity, and determination to make a difference in the world are the reasons this book exists. You remind us all that creativity knows no bounds, and age is never a limitation.

To my family, thank you for your unwavering support and encouragement. Your belief in me and my vision fuelled my determination to bring this book to life.

To my parents, who nurtured my curiosity and fostered my love for learning, I owe my deepest gratitude.

I extend special thanks to the mentors, educators, and friends who have guided me through my own journey of growth and discovery. Your wisdom and insights have been invaluable, shaping not only this book but also my understanding of what it means to lead with purpose.

To the incredible team who helped bring this book from concept to completion, thank you for your expertise and dedication. From editing and designing to providing feedback and shaping the narrative, your contributions have elevated this work to something I am truly proud of.

To the readers of this book, thank you for trusting me to guide you on your entrepreneurial journey. Your decision to pick up *IGNITE-INNOVATE-LEAD* is a testament to your commitment to growth and innovation. I am honoured to be a small part of your path to success.

Finally, to the countless entrepreneurs—young and old—whose stories I have had the privilege to learn from and share, thank you for proving that the spirit of innovation is alive and thriving. Your resilience and creativity are a source of endless inspiration.

This book is a tribute to everyone who believes in the power of ideas, the courage to take risks, and the determination to lead. Thank you for being part of this journey. Together, we can ignite sparks of innovation, create meaningful change, and inspire the leaders of tomorrow.

With immense gratitude,

Priya Ratan Sharma

www.ingramcontent.com/pod-product-compliance
Lightning Source LLC
Chambersburg PA
CBHW071653240526
45469CB00021B/2275